LOCK

The Complete Guide for Beginners to Master the Art of Lock Picking Skills and Avoid Beginner Mistakes

Joseph
McKnight

Copyright © 2021 Joseph McKnight

All rights reserved.

It is not legal to reproduce, duplicate, or transmit any part of this document by either electronic means or in printed format. Recording of this publication is strictly prohibited

Disclaimer

The information in this book is based on personal experience and anecdotal evidence. Although the author has made every attempt to achieve an accuracy of the information gathered in this book, they make no representation or warranties concerning the accuracy or completeness of the contents of this book. Your circumstances may not be suited to some illustrations in this book.

The author disclaims any liability arising directly or indirectly from the use of this book. Readers are encouraged to seek Medical. Accounting, legal, or professional help when required.

This guide is for informational purposes only, and the author does not accept any responsibilities for any liabilities resulting from the use of this information. While every attempt has been made to verify the information provided here, the author cannot assume any responsibility for errors, inaccuracies or omission.

Printed in the United States of America

Table of Contents

INTRODUCTION i
CHAPTER ONE 1
Operation of a standard Lock..1
   The most common locks...1
   Distinct forms of cylinders 3
CHAPTER TWO 5
Types of Locks 5
   Pin Cylinder Locks 8
   Lever Locks 10
   Wafer Locks 13
   Warded Locks 16
CHAPTER THREE 18
The Principles of Lock picking 18
   The standard of lock picking..18
   Interior view of a plug 22
   Illustration of non-alignment of the wells in a shell...22
   Sectional View of a plug in the shear line 23

Understanding of the pin passing the shear line 27
CHAPTER FOUR..29
The Components of a Lock cylinder....................29
   Lock cylinder components 29
   Sectional view of an European cylinder 33
   The essential things to keep in mind 39
CHAPTER FIVE...41
The anti-picking pins 41
   The difficulty in interpreting feedback.............42
   The most common anti-picking pins 43
   The function of an anti-picking pin 44
   Overcome the anti-picking pins........................45
   Using the mushroom pin to apply tension to a plug 47
CHAPTER SIX 49
Picks for pin tumbler locks 49
   Tools for raking 50
   Tools for single pin picking 51

CHAPTER SEVEN 55
Buying tools 55
    The fineness of the tool 56
    The importance of blade thickness 57
    The importance of blade height 59
    The strength of the tool..60
    The ergonomics of the tool 61
CHAPTER EIGHT 63
The different tools 63
    The tension tools 63
    Tension tool in action 65
    When is a tension too much? 66
    When is a tension too little?................................67
    When is a tension correct?..................................68
    Making conventional tools...................................69
    How to tension 73
    Inserting the tension tool at the bottom of the keyway...76
    Use of conventional tension tools 78

CHAPTER NINE 81
Making your own tools..81
  The tools you will need..81
  Steps to make homemade picks 87
CHAPTER TEN 89
Lock Picking Techniques 89
  The raking technique 91
  Using raking tools 92
  Applying the appropriate raking tension.........97
  Making use of single pin picking tools 98
  Usefulness of the raking anti-picking pins.......101
  Making Use of Single Pin picking tools 104
  How to apply the appropriate tension when single pin picking 108
CHAPTER ELEVEN 110
Common Lock Picking Mistakes........................110
  Picking locks that are too hard...........................110
  Improper Tools...114
  Relying on Transparent Locks...........................116
  Concentrating on too much Raking 118

Do Not Practice Constantly	120
CONCLUSION	123
ABOUT THE AUTHOR	126

INTRODUCTION

This approach simply indicates that you can highlight the disadvantages of a physical security system if you clearly comprehend lock manipulation. This will simply be of assistance in safeguarding the vulnerabilities that exist and maintaining the troubleshooting professionals and professionalism of locksmiths.

Due to this, we made an available introduction of different techniques of lock picking to customers. In other words, these interested locksmiths and customers will clearly comprehend the basics and techniques of lock picking.

Before we go into details, always keep in mind that the already bought and used lock picking tools are legal in many countries, as long as you only use it on locks that you are in possession of, or with the explicit permission of the lock owner. This also simply indicates that one is committing a crime if he or she does not follow any of the two steps mentioned above to open locks.

CHAPTER ONE

Operation of a standard Lock

The most common locks

The flat key locks and the paracentric pinned locks are the most common locks. This is not strictly discussing about the total number of locks, since the lock is a term which can be defined as an entire mechanism dedicated to the opening and closure of the door or other mechanism.

As a result of the fact that we are just focusing on the methods of non-destructive opening in this presentation, we are fascinated only about the lock cylinder and not the lock case or the complete lock.

Nonetheless, if you want to be more comprehensible and avoid repetitions, we will concentrate more on the terms, locks or cylinders.

Distinct forms of cylinders

The different forms of cylinders include the following;

- Round cylinders. These types of cylinders are usually mounted on dead bolts.
- And the European kind cylinders. These types of cylinders are often fitted with lock case being established inside the door.

For your notice, the two different forms of cylinders, that is, the round cylinders and European kind cylinders have identical operation. Besides, the needs of both cylinders must be thoroughly comprehended before you learn how to pick them.

CHAPTER TWO

Types of Locks

Knowing the kinds or types of locks to pick is very important. Before you pick a lock, you clearly need to understand the different types of locks.

Before we go into details, let us turn our focus on the different kinds of locks, then we can know what they offer. As we all know that there many kinds of locks out there, it is better we concentrate on the most popular and the kind of locks you are likely to experience in the world today. As a matter of fact, one of these locks we will mention might be the first lock you will pick.

You might discover that things may get complex since we need to clearly explain whether it is the lock mechanism or lock housing we are talking about. Let us take for example, 'padlock' is clearly the housing of a lock mechanism, although you can make use of various different locking mechanisms with the padlock. In this chapter, we will be concentrating on the locking mechanism, how the locks functions especially inside, and the kind of picks you need considering the internal mechanism.

Even though there are various kinds of specialist lock mechanisms, there are only five primary kinds of locks you need to learn, since these are the ones you may experience in your life on a daily basis. The five kinds of locks are the pin cylinder locks, the lever locks, the wafer locks, the warded locks, and the disc detainer locks.

Pin Cylinder Locks

The most ancient locking mechanism is the pin cylinder locking mechanism. The wooden locks found at the pyramids of ancient Egypt almost looks like the pin cylinder locks. Nonetheless, Linus Yale popularized it and also patented this specific lock in 1851. As a result of the success of his locks, a lot of individuals currently refer to these specific locks as 'Yale' locks. If you must know, the pin cylinder locks are mostly used today.

In terms of the principle, it is quite simple. There is a plug or central core that must rotate before the lock can be opened. A series of pins usually prevents the plug from turning which simply indicates that the plug is obstructed. When you insert the correct key, the pairs of driver pins and key pins lines splits up along the top side of the plug where it comes in contact with the housing of the lock. This is otherwise known as the shear line. The plug will be able to turn and the lock open once this has occurred. If you are lock picker, you must ensure that the pin pairs splits along the shear line in order to enable the plug rotate or turn and the lock open.

Lever Locks

Lock pickers usually see the lever locks as the next progression. The reason is that it is popular and also offer a certain challenge. The lever locks are the second most used locks in the universe. Robert Barron, who was an English man attributed and designed the lever locks in 1778.

In terms of the principle, the lever locks possesses a cut-aways or gates which must be lifted to distinctive heights to let the bolt stump to move and also make the door open. When the key is inserted and also turned, all the levers will be lifted to the correct height.

The bolt thrower is the last one on one of the cuts on the key. Also, when you turn the key, you will notice that the levers are raised and the bolt is moved by the bolt thrower.

Keep in mind that you can find the lever lock mechanisms in padlocks or even domestic front doors. You can also use two pieces of wire to pick simple lever locks. One of the wires is used to apply pressure on the bolt, while the other wire is used to life the levers. When you use a tension wrench to apply tension to the bolt, you are directly creating a small ledge. When you must have created the ledge, that is, a fraction of a millimeter, you are directly lifting the levers till they are placed on the ledge.

In summary, assuming you intend to know how to pick this specific type of locks, it is either you find yourself lucky with an easy mechanism or a few bent wires and also a makeshift tension wrench. Nonetheless, try to be watchful when you make use of any objects such as the bobby pin, knife, or even the credit card to pick or wrench, since you may cause damage to the lock or the object.

Wafer Locks

Even though the wafer locks are not as popular as the lever locks and the pin cylinder locks, it is still significant because you can use it in millions of motor vehicles. Apart from the point just mentioned, you can use the wafer locks on drawers, padlocks, and even lockers.

Philo Felter first recorded the wafer lock in 1868. His lock was double bitted, which simply indicates that the lock possesses two sets of wafers.

In terms of the principle, the wafer locks is familiar to the pin cylinders locks. In other words, you can use it to push obstructions into the housing of the lock which certainly prevents the plug from rotating. Unlike other kinds of licks that uses pins, the wafer locks uses wafers which is a series of flat single pieces of metal. You can have access to either the double-sided or single wafer locks but if you want to comprehend either of them, you will need to start with the single sided. You can find the single sided locks in a locker.

Typically, a spring pushes the wafers through the plug and sticks out into the housing at the bottom of the lock. The plug is then prevented from rotating and the lock will open. When you insert the correct key, you will notice the wafers lifting up, although they will push up into the housing.

In terms of the design, the wafer locks and the pin cylinder locks are similar. But when you intend to use the wafer locks, you must consider the same pick sets. You can apply the required pressure by using a tension wrench. After that, enter a pick before picking the wafers.

Warded Locks

Currently, the warded locks are among the least used locks. Most times, the warded locks are used on items or historic properties with the aim of maintaining the old aesthetic. The lack of security is the basic reason for their scarcity.

Even though this type of lock houses an easy turning mechanism, it is still vulnerable to an easy attack since they are locked properly. As a matter of fact, you can use a few bent wires to tackle various warded locks. In other words, you do not have to use the picking tools or tension wrench to tackle the warded locks.

Finally, the warded lock picks is a recognized and easy lock pick set that can deal with majority of warded locks in use.

CHAPTER THREE

The Principles of Lock picking

The standard of lock picking

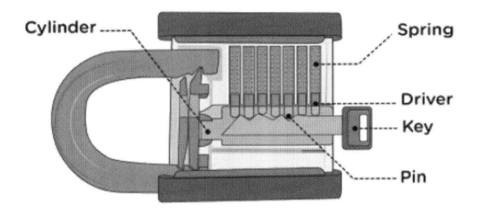

Assuming that there are areas that do not possess setbacks from the approximation, the perfect instance is the locksmith. You can even exploit the most subtle vulnerability as long as one takes enough time to comprehend and investigate it. This method simply shows how effective a specific system that is theoretically ideal can be negated.

Discovering and exploiting these vulnerabilities to successfully run the locking mechanism is the basic essence of the lock manipulation.

If you want to fully comprehend the first of these vulnerabilities, simply think of an ideal straight line on which a specific number of holes are aligned. The springs and the pin stacks of the cylinder are positioned in these wells.

A common alignment discovered in all pinned locking devices is the theoretical line. Keep in mind that every pin well is ideally aligned on the same axis. Also, keep in mind that the locksmith is fortunate since the ideal alignment only exists in the field of pure geometry.

If you want to face the real world, you will discover that even the most advanced milling machinery cannot mill or even drill an ideal linear line for the pin walls.

Therefore, we often have the pin wells misaligned and at times, have different diameters. Even though these differences do not exceed a few tenths of a millimeter, it is adequate or satisfactory for the entire principle of lock picking to function.

As a matter of fact, assuming every pin were aligned in an ideally straight line, certainly every pin would simultaneously contact with the shell and plug. Due to this, it would be not be possible especially when picking the cylinder to determine in what order to set the pins.

Interior view of a plug

Let us assume you intend to launch or open the cylinder, you are advised to set the binding pins at the shear line till you notice them all correctly placed. You can then open the cylinder just as the original key had been used.

Illustration of non-alignment of the wells in a shell

Keep in mind that not all wells are aligned on the exact axis. When you apply tension on the plug, certainly the pin wells will not be ideally aligned.

Also, the single pin blocks the rotation in the shell rather than all of the pins.

Sectional View of a plug in the shear line

As the plug rotates, the driver pins stay in the pin wells of the shell. Also, the key pins found above the shear line stay in the plug during rotation.

Certainly, the theory will need long hours of practice to fully comprehend the feedback of sensations. In addition, the manufacturing defects in many cases are so subtle that numerous pins bind at the exact time when a turning force is applied on the plug.

Let us assume you fully comprehend this section on the principles for lock picking. We can move further on how you can test how lock producers can attempt to defeat a lockpicker.

Section of a plug wells that are not perfectly aligned

The shear line is usually on both sides of the one driver pin, but only when there is an application of a rotation to the plug. Besides, while you pick the lock and apply the tension on the plug with the help of a suitable tension tool, the friction occurs with a single pin at a time; since it is trapped between the plug and the shell.

At this stage, the other pins can easily set in place; although these pins may go back to their rightful position at anytime, since the friction does not hold them or it is not in contact with the walls of the wells in the shell or plug.

In order to fully comprehend the pin that is bound by the friction, you will be required to acquire or obtain the necessary touch.

When the shear line has the binding pin, you will certainly feel a click sound or clear snap. If you do not release the tension, then this pin will not move any further.

Certainly, the pin remains there once it is placed. The reason is that a small amount must have been rotated by the plug. In other words, the pin stack will be prevented from going back to the resting position or rightful position.

Understanding of the pin passing the shear line

The plug rotates one or two degrees once the pin is placed at the shear line. The degree(s) rotating will help to bind the next pin with friction. Also, the pin is prevented by this friction to go back to the position of rest beneath the pressure of the spring.

In addition, the first binding pin does not longer exist as a hindrance between the shell and the plug once it is placed at the shear line.

So, the under pressure plug from the tension tool rotates one or two degrees, till the opposition from the next holding pin is found by the rotation.

CHAPTER FOUR

The Components of a Lock cylinder

Lock cylinder components

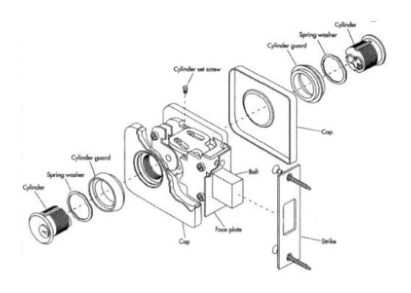

We will begin with the vocabulary and use of each part of a common lock to fully understand the non-destructive techniques in picking a lock.

Having this knowledge will enable you to use a specific technical vocabulary. Therefore, it gives you and I the chance to comprehend how a lock operates and also how you can open a lock without the firing key.

External components of a cylinder

The external components of a cylinder includes; the shell, the cam, the plug, and the C-clips.

1. The Shell

A motionless part that can fit to the door or even the lock case is otherwise known as the shell.

2. The Cam

This specific component of a cylinder is usually directly connected to the plug. Besides, it turns with the lock case and inside the door. Finally, this specific component of a cylinder, that is, the cam set the motion to the door locking mechanism.

3. The Plug

The rotating section where you are able to insert your key is otherwise known as the plug. When you turn the key to unlock or lock, the plug triggers the cam.

4. The C-clips

Any thin C-shaped strip of metal around the rear of the plug is otherwise known as the C-clips. This specific component of a cylinder prevents the plug from popping out especially when a key is inserted.

Sectional view of an European cylinder

The sectional view of a European cylinder includes the following;

1. The Key pins

The key pins and the driver pins are always in contact when both pins are at their base. Since the key pins and the driver pins have different lengths, you can find the right combination of the key by aligning them at the shear line and permitting the opening of the cylinder.

In order to minimize friction with the key since it is inserted into the keyway, simply round off the tip of the key pin.

2. The Driver pins

The driver pins, the key pins, and the springs, all come in direct contact. Besides, they all pass through the shell and plug. An obstacle is formed by the pins, but only if there are no key inserted. This will automatically prevent the cylinder from opening.

Nonetheless, when you insert the correct key, the driver pins will continue to stay in the rightful position which is inside the lock shell. The plug can then allow the mechanism close or open by rotating.

3. The pin wells

The pin wells go through the shell and lock plug. The reason why the pin wells exist is that it guides the springs and pins. It also, theoretically aligns in a straight line that goes through the axis of the shell and plug.

Facing the real world, the positioning of the pin wells consist of extremely small variations that result to the few tenths of millimeters. That being said, the basis for picking a lock is basically these small imperfections.

4. The Springs

Since the springs are usually forced in the pin chambers, it definitely let the pins to move through the plug and shell. When a pick or key is inserted into the cylinder, a force is put on the pins.

Once the biting of the key is introduced to the lock, the force of the springs on the pins automatically reads it. Also, once the key is removed from the cylinder, the pins will automatically go back to its initial or rightful position.

5. The well plugs

The brass or steel makes the well plugs. Also, the well plugs are usually sealed to the ends of the pin wells, but only if there is an introduction from both the springs and pins.

6. The shear line

The shear line can also be referred as the physical separation of the shells and plug. When the breaks between the key pins and driver are aligned with the shear line, the cylinder automatically opens. Due to this statement, the lock is able to open and the plug is able to turn while remaining attached to a shell. Keep in mind that the shell uses a secured ring to hold the plug and shell. The shear line also prevents the shell from being withdrawn from the plug.

7. The clutch

The clutch can be found at the back of the cylinder, that is, inside the cam. What is the basic duty of the clutch? Well, it links or connects the plug with the cam on the side of the inserted key.

8. The Driver pin or key pin break

The physical line of division between a driver pin and a key pin associated with it is otherwise known as the driver pin or key pin break.

The essential things to keep in mind

A static component is always included in the lock cylinder. This static component is otherwise known as the shell and the plug. Keep in mind that the plug is a mobile component.

The cam is able to close and open the lock since the plug rotates.

Tip: The plug is unable to rotate when there is no key inserted. The reason for this is that the rotation is hindered by the driver pins. The plug is also unable to rotate if the key inserted is incorrect. The reason for this is that the rotation is hindered by either the key pins or the driver pins.

Tip: The line of division between the driver pins and key pins is made parallel with the line of division between the shell and plug, but only if the key inserted is correct. Due to this reason, the plug is able to rotate freely.

CHAPTER FIVE

The anti-picking pins

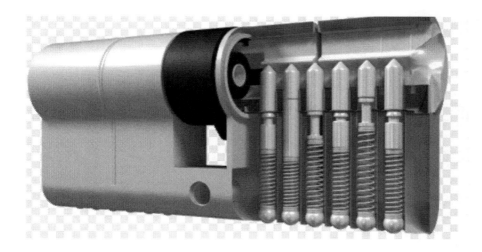

Manufacturers or producers use numerous methods of preventing or at least, delaying the manipulation of their cylinder. This includes the attempt to distort the feedback alleged during picking. It also includes the attempt to dampen the insertion of picking tools in the plug.

The difficulty in interpreting feedback

The tool that transmits the feedback to the picker lets him to be aware of a pin set or not. To prevent yourself from being misled especially in picking the lock key, consider using the anti-picking pin, which is otherwise known as the security pins. The purpose of the security pins or the anti-picking pins is to allow manufacturers use it as key pins. Keep in mind that the anti-picking pins are often used as driver pins.

The most common anti-picking pins

The most common anti-picking pins you can find currently are; the mushroom pin, the spool pin, and the serrated pin.

Irrespective of the type and number of anti-picking pin you are using, know that the cylinder makes it possible. It may occur that there is a similarity between the driver pins of a cylinder and the anti-picking pins of different forms. It is not common for a cylinder to have only one or two, while the remaining pins are standard in nature.

You should note that the most frequent in cylinders are the spool type pins, while the pins that are not very common on European cylinders are the serrated and mushroom pins.

The function of an anti-picking pin

The functions of this feature are as follows;

- Force applied to the pin
- Direction of rotation on the plug
- In the opposite direction of the plug rotation, there is the rotational force which is similar to

the force needed to change the direction of the pin.

Overcome the anti-picking pins

In theory, you can find it very easy or simple in overcoming anti-picking pins. But when you intend to practice it, it can be tough or difficult.

Overcoming this feature is simply applying a very low pressure on the tension tool and the binding tool. The reason you need to apply pressure on the tension tool is to hold the tension tool in the rightful place.

Applying pressure on the anti-picking pin will certainly make the plug rotate a few degrees, although you may discover that the plug will counter-rotate; but only if you stroke your tool on the pins repeatedly.

Also, applying pressure on this feature and using the tension tool to fluctuate the tension can let the plug to counter-rotate till you can listen or even feel the slight click of the pin in the shear line. Besides, this will let the plug rotate a few degrees.

You should be totally convinced that it is not the anti-picking bait, rather it is the shear-line. Once you press the pin for the second time, it will not likely go back to the rotor backwards anymore. In other words, the overlapping wells of the stator and rotor will permanently block it.

Using the mushroom pin to apply tension to a plug

It is so obvious that when you apply pressure to any of the anti-picking pins, there is a slight rotation on the plug. There is this impression by the rotation that the pin is set at the shear line.

Nonetheless, it is very easy to comprehend the positioning of the pin on the shear line and this trick. Furthermore, when the anti-picking pin is not properly positioned at the shear line, but depressed; you are very likely to discover that any application of pressure on the pin with a pick will lead to the plug counter-rotating.

CHAPTER SIX

Picks for pin tumbler locks

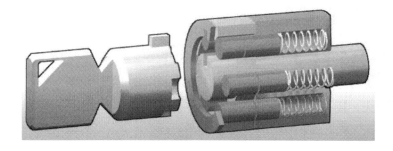

Now, that you have an idea about the tension tools, let us turn our focus at the picks. Picking kits usually possess a wide diversity of pick forms.

While at times, this variety can be perplexing, you can find it easy to navigate.

Tools for raking

The user can be allowed to quickly open a cylinder if he or she uses the raking tools and not the anti-picking tools. The heads of these raking tools should be able to act simultaneously on various pins.

There are two sub-categories of the raking tools;

- The tools which comes along with the teeth. It is often regarded or otherwise known as the rakes, cry rakes, or the five mountains.
- The tools which comes along with a particular curves that act on the pins. Since it possesses the snake-like forms, it is otherwise known as the snake rakes.

Tools for single pin picking

When it concerns designing to act on just a single pin at a time, it is the known as the most popular tools. The tools for single pin picking are very different from the raking tools. Why? The former can be of assistance in overcoming anti-picking pins. Besides, the tools for single pin picking are completely necessary for launching good quality cylinders.

The tools for single pin picking have three different kinds:

- **The hook or feeler pick**

The most widespread and recognized tool is the feeler hook-picks. It is also known as the most effective tools for probing. There are several varieties of the hook including the curves. You can deal with many types of situations if you select a tool with an average curve.

- **The half-diamond picks**

Since this type of pick has a rounded shape, it can prevent the pick from getting caught on the wafer. In general terms, the wafer locks are used on low security locks like the vehicles and mail boxes. Once you rake or use the hook picks, you can successfully open these kinds of locks.

- **The Half-moon pick**

You can get different forms of all the tools mentioned above, except from the fact that the feelers possess variations in the curvature.

There are various kits especially the two sided picking tools in this specific tool. With two pin or wafer rows, you can simultaneously pick two rows of pins on a lock, but only if the tension tool is fitted to create more space.

CHAPTER SEVEN

Buying tools

Rather than making your own tools, it is better and even easier to buy or purchase your tools. These tools are affordable to buy. A great value is added by these quality and materials you bought and it is better than any handmade tools.

Before you consider selecting your picks, ensure to pick any of these three elements listed below;

The fineness of a tool, the ergonomics, and the strength.

The fineness of the tool

When neither of the height of the pick blade and thickness of the steel used is considered, then you are directly getting the fineness of the tool.

The steel thickness should not surpass 0.8 or even 0.7 mm. It will be more difficult or tough to man over in or even access the keyway if you are making use of thicker tools. Due to this, the feedback will even be much tougher to interpret.

The tools which are considered the thinnest are known to be in the range of 0.3 and 0.4 mm thick. While these kinds of tools may be considered as the ideal tools, they do offer the least amount of strength.

The importance of blade thickness

You can insert a thin tool into all keyway profiles and prevent the plug and tool from having too much friction.

If you intend to purchase a tool, try to consider and focus on the height of the blades. As a matter of fact, a significant proportion of tools are designed for the American market. The U.S locks are suited to this kind of tools. Also, the Atlantic part of the world mostly uses this type of tool. For your notice, the European locks are not suitable or adequate to this type of tools because users may feel disappointed using it.

So, it is better if you are in possession of tools that are designed for European locks. The height of the blade should not surpass 3mm and if possible, should be finer for greater maneuverability in the cylinder keyway. Since they are known to be very thin, you can make use of them in the U. S locks without experiencing any problem.

The importance of blade height

Pick adapted to the American market can make the tool difficult to handle or use as a result of the height. Also, pick adapted for the European market can allow manipulation of the last pin as a result of the low height of the blade.

The strength of the tool

Certainly, if you intend to purchase, it can be difficult to access this point.

If you are yet to be convinced, simply try to select tools which were initially sold by American or European producers. You can also select tools when you are certain of the specifics of the steel used in manufacturing the tools. Generally, these will be of evidence in providing better quality, unlike tools produced from the Asian part of the universe.

The ergonomics of the tool

Apart from the visual aspect, the ergonomics of the tools' handle is very critical. As a matter of fact, the grip and feel when picking is determined by the ergonomics. Due to this, it is not recommended to consider using handles with soft rubber or plastic or even wide handles.

The tendency of suppressing the feedback is quite high. This then proves counter-productive for selecting the lock. If you want an effective lock manipulation, then you need to fully rely on the feedback given by the tool on the pins.

In disparity, if you are choosing hard plastic handles or metal handles, just keep in mind that the heat shrink rubbing can be perfect in acquiring or obtaining a good feel for the opening. Nonetheless, your fingers can get tired easily and even become painful to hold at the time of extended picking sessions if you are making use of a thin bare metal handle.

CHAPTER EIGHT

The different tools

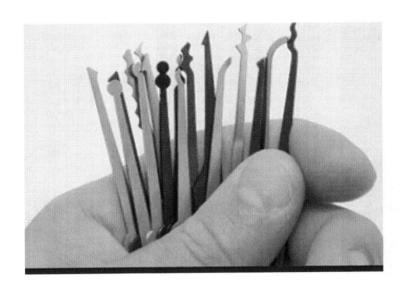

The tension tools

Unlike tools such as the feeler picks, you do not need to put your full attention to the tension tool. Also, producers of this specific tool have considered that one or two kinds of tool are sufficient in the pick sets they sell.

This may be a mistake, since the cases we have discovered have shown that the selection of tension tool, the application of pressure, and the position in the lock is much more crucial than the pick used to apply pressure on the pins.

From the explanation seen above, exerting a rotational force on the rotor is the basic role of the tension wrench. This will enable the shear between the shell and plug to get hold of the pins.

And can gradually be lowered till the shear line stay in the rightful position.

Tension tool in action

Note: Driver pins need to be brought to the shear line if it is already trapped between the shell and plug. This will make the cylinder to open.

The driver pin is no longer trapped between the shell and plug if it is already brought to the shear line.

The application of tension to the plug by the tension tool is the key element to lock picking. As a result of the fact that it is not sufficient to apply a regular mechanical strength, the feedback from the picker interprets that it must be consistently adjusted and controlled.

When is a tension too much?

When all pins are blocked, then you are applying too much tension. When you apply too much tension, you would not be able to find the binding pin. The chances of a pick breaking are high as long as it applies too much amount of force to set a key pin. Assuming you just got know about lockpicking, and you are experiencing so many issues with opening your first locks; well, keep in mind that the issue is extreme tension applied to the plug.

When is a tension too little?

We have so far discussed about the negative impacts of too much tension, now let us turn our concentration to when the tension is too little. You may experience the pins not binding and setting at the shear line between the shell and plug.

Besides, perceiving which pin is binding may not be possible if the tension is too little. The pins may not remain in position once they are set.

When is a tension correct?

Any tension that allows the first binding pin to be held by friction on the walls of the pin well while staying free enough to be set in position by the pick is otherwise known as the correct tension.

The tension applied must be light before it can allow a pin to be placed in the plug. The feedback from the tension will be lost if it is too strong. Also, the cylinder opening will be unknown if the tension is too strong.

Certainly, there are a few cylinders that need more tension. If you must know, a correct tension is a tension that enables the picker has access to maximum feedback when selecting the cylinder.

Making conventional tools

The conventional tools simply comprises of one metal strip curved to a small L-shape. The keyway of the plug is in possession of the inserted smaller length of the L while the longer length of the L shape is in possession of the exerted rotational pressure.

The tension tool need to be securely set at the top or bottom of the keyway in order to allow the lock to be picked or even let enough room for the pick to be inserted in the keyway.

Certainly, there are only two positions that give enough space for the pick to be entered to set the pins.

There are two kinds of conventional tension tools:

Irrespective of the fact that the tension tool is placed at the bottom or top of the keyway, size and thickness of the smaller length of the L shape will vary to give maximum fit. A length of about 1 cm is ideal for the top of the keyway, that is, the opposite of pins side. The serrations or small teeth in the end of the tension tool that has already been placed in the keyway will give additional grip.

The length for the bottom of the keyway should have not more than 1 or 2 millimeters inserted in the keyway. The reason is to prevent the length from getting in touch with the first pin. The top of the keyway tools should be thicker than it, so you can properly insert it.

Views evaluating the end of the tension tool for the bottom and top of the keyway

It is not important to have the length of the longer end of the tension tool, although you should try to avoid the lengths of around 5 cm to reach out to the door frame or handle when selecting a lock.

The tension tool, on the other hand, transmits useful information to the individual picking. Most especially, in terms of the small changes in rotation of the plug and the movement of security pins that need some counter rotation in certain situations.

Due to this, focusing on tension tools of not flexible metals is better, since it can give maximum feedback.

In summary, while the L-shaped tension tools are the most common, it is very possible to limit the number of tension tools if you make use of the Z-shaped tension tools. If you follow this method, you can have a tension tool with an option of two ends to insert at the bottom or top of the plug keyway.

How to tension

1. First of all, you can tension from the edge of the keyway.

You are simply practicing the most conventional and easiest position for the tension tool if you consider this method, although you should keep in mind that this method is not the most effective.

Certainly, the space available to insert the pick is limited if you insert the tension tool at the edge of the keyway. Nonetheless, you can pick relatively easy cylinders since this technique is very useful.

For the tension tool, on the other hand, it seems to be very useful especially when it is inserted at the edge of the keyway to open the cylinder.

2. Secondly, you can tension from the bottom of the keyway.

The most effective method of tensioning a cylinder is to tension from the bottom of the keyway, although when you rake the pins, it can be too complex to open.

This configuration simply indicates that the tension tool is set at the bottom of the keyway and also inserted so that the first pin and the end of the tension tool do not reach out to each other. In other words, it blocks or hinders it when it needs to be selected.

Inserting the tension tool at the bottom of the keyway

This basic technique has a huge advantage? What is this advantage? Well, majority of the keyway are free to insert a pick. Nonetheless, this particular technique needs a wider selection of tension tools than the edge of the keyway, since the perfect tool to use fully relies on the depth of the first pin in the keyway and the width of the keyway. Due to this, having broader selection of tension tools is better, most especially in terms of dealing with most of the typical keyways.

Irrespective of the fact that it possesses a slight drawback, it is recommended that you start practicing especially with the use of inserting the tension tool at the bottom of the keyway.

Certainly, a lot of lock pickers start with the top of the keyway tensioning, but when these lock pickers experience more complicated or difficult cylinder locks, they will be required to modify their habits.

It is better to put more effort especially in starting directly with bottom tensioning.

Use of conventional tension tools

In most picking kits sold by retailers, one or more tension tools are typically provided or offered. But keep in mind that these retailers will not always be well apposite to narrow locks since they are often too thick.

Nonetheless, making them very affordable from windshield wiper inserts is very much possible. There is usually a metal blade about 50 cm long with impressive rigidity just within the rubber blade of an already used windshield wiper blade. You should be in possession of an impressive tension tool that can be compared with those sold by numerous or various manufacturers if you cut into length of 6 to 7 cm.

You can bend 1 to 2 mm at the end and also field it if necessary to fit the keyways, but only if you consider using the tension tools in the bottom of the keyway tensioning.

Lastly, If you use a small triangular file to cut teeth or serrations into the end sides, you can certainly make improve these tension tools. In other words, these tension tools will fit securely in the keyway.

CHAPTER NINE

Making your own tools

The tools you will need

Making your own tools is not really necessary, because there is a wide range of good quality of tools in the market. Nonetheless, opening locks with tools you did with your hands can be satisfying.

The types of tools that will be required in making your own tools are as follows;

- Hacksaw blades or a masonry trowel
- A small bench grinder
- Protective goggles
- Glue and paper
- An iron
- A glass of water

For home made picks, the most classic material you should consider using is the metal saw blades. This metal saw blades are made from good durable and rigid steel. It also has a thickness in the range of 0.6 mm to 0.8 mm. it is also adequate, despite the fact that it is a bit thick.

Nonetheless, the perfect thing about using the metal plate of a masonry trowel is that is it of better quality than the normal trade. It is also used by renowned pickers. As a matter of fact, this steel is ideally suited to creating picks which could either come from the point of view of thickness or rigidity and strength.

The strapping tool can be used to close feller gauges or pallets to measure the clearance of the spark plugs. It should be in the range of 0.4 mm and 0.6 mm.

Once you are in possession of the steel for your picks, you need to go to the internet to print a template and watch over the scale that is printed.

Immediately the template must have been printed to scale, it is compulsory for you to cut and paste the template on the metal.

Cutting a rectangle of paper around the printed pick template is the perfect tip for the pasting. You simply transfer the paper before soaking the rectangle into the water for a few minutes, precisely five minutes. After that, apply the paper into the blade and ensure that the blade displays the printed side.

Also, for the ink to be deposited into the metal blade, simply skip a very hot iron over the paper. By this period, you should be in possession of a real printed transfer.

Once you are through with this transfer, you can make use of the bench grinder to gradually crop the metal. At regular intervals, simply watch over the blade in cold water to cool in and prevent the metal to get easily broken.

If you have an unavailable bench grinder, it is sufficient to make use of an easy metal file since it requires a lot more time and patience. Immediately you are through with the shape of the tool, use a file or sandpaper to de-burr the edges. You should witness the pick not being able to catch the interior of the lock keyway.

Lastly, you can have a more comfortable grip from heat-shrink tubing by making a handle. You can just heat this for some minutes in a heat gun or a hot oven. This will enable the handle form properly around the blade of the pick.

Cutting sleeves from plastic, metal, glue, rivet, weld, or wood is another solution you can consider in having a thickened handle.

Steps to make homemade picks

Step One: Select the material.

Step two: Paste the printed template on the blade. Once you are through with soaking the paper template, simply place it on the blade.

Step three: Transfer of template print. Once you are through with using an iron to heat the paper template, simply get rid of it from the blade. The blade should have the printed ink

Step four: Trimming the tool. Gradually, the tool is trimmed.

Step five: Creating the handle. The handle is in possession of the fixed heat shrink tube.

CHAPTER TEN

Lock Picking Techniques

Once you must have fully comprehended the operation of a lock pin, let us totally focus on practicing the technique.

You must first begin from using a low priced cylinder from DIY store if you want to open your first lock. Also, ensure to be in possession of different keys so that you can practice on distinctive key combination.

You should not start practicing this technique with more complicated cylinders apart from some of the European models. You will certainly struggle to progress and comprehend the feedback the lock is passing to you. But when you fully understand the opening of the low price cylinders, then these more complicated locks will become useful.

Besides, you should not focus on already used cylinders or cylinders that have already been placed to gates or doors. These types of cylinders are only meant for pickers who are very experienced, especially those that can break a tool in the lock.

The raking technique

Setting numerous cylinder pins without having the need to separately probe each pin in the cylinder is the basic technique of raking. The action of the rake usually set the pins progressively and shows its evidence in two cases;

1. The pins set at the shear line are allowed by the raking action if the cylinder fails to include anti-picking pins.
2. The difference in key pin size is reduced when the pin biting is

relatively flat. You should experience that the locks is in possession of the keys pins with a greater variant of height are very tough to rake open.

These two cases are certainly perfect for raking.

Using raking tools

Just as we gave a full explanation in the description of tools, the two kinds of raking tools are common;

- City rakes that are in possession of cuts at distinctive heights in order to set pins of differing heights

- Snake rakes that work hand in hand in the exact principle, although with curves of distinctive heights.

As a matter of fact, there is similarity in terms of efficiency in both tools. Besides, the use cases are identical. Nonetheless, the snake rakes are preferred to the city rakes, since their rounded form glides inside the cylinder. On the other hand, the city rakes are more harsh or rough on the pins.

When you rake for a few minutes with any of them, you will certainly notice what we have explained above. Note:

if you intend to get rid of the brass dust, simply click the lock face on a flat surface.

Nonetheless, irrespective of what we recommend, you can decide on any of the tools you want for your cylinder.

Due to this, you can simply comprehend that the action on the pins must be uniform and even powered by changing the location of the tool on the pins.

Nonetheless, the combination of pin heights determines the existing difference between the highest set pin at the shear line and the lowest set pin at the shear line. Therefore, you are advised to begin with the rake placed on a parallel line along with the pins, and you are required to use different angles with the rake if the lock is unable to open even after moving the rake over the pins back and forth.

Also, always remember that raking generally enables you to attempt every single combination within your capabilities with the rake very quickly.

Let us assume that after some minutes using the correct tension to rake, and your cylinder is unable to open; it simply indicates that the cylinder is in possession of the anti-picking pins or that the height difference between the lowest pin and the highest pin in relation to the curve of the tool is not good enough.

What you can only do in such situation is to complete the picking by making use of a hook pick. You must have set some pins in place during the raking.

Make sure you do not release the tension tool assuming you modify your raking tool or pick, since it might go back to the pins to the position they often rest.

Applying the appropriate raking tension

Even though it is strongly recommended that you begin to enlighten yourself on how to tension a plug from the bottom of the keyway, it is better if you rake to tension from the center or even the top of the keyway.

Tensioning a plug from the center or top of the keyway can automatically enable the tension tool to serve as a guide for the rake; although you have to slide against the tension to have access to more regular mechanical action that can be effective on the pins.

If you need to change the position of the tension tool, then simply change it to the bottom or top of the keyway in order to access different action.

Making use of single pin picking tools

The single pin picking tools usually possess flexible and minimal pressure on the tension tool, since it typically lets the simultaneous setting of numerous pins.

Let us assume that as a rake passes over the pins, you can hear the pins responding to the spring pressure; it simply means that there is an application of the correct tension. Nonetheless, when there is no application of tension and the pins are not even placed at the shear line, you can still hear this spring pinging.

That being said, you can make use of the following exercise to locate the correct tension you are required to apply;

1. On your tension tool, simply release the tension. After that, pay attention to any of the pins which may go back to their rest position.

2. Pass the rake back and forth over the pins a few times. This will enable you to hear the sound produced by the pins beneath the spring pressure.
3. Continue with these steps till you can get both the sound produced by the pins when the rake is passed over and the sound of the pins produced when they go back to their rest position.

You should be in possession of the correct tension that must be applied once you have the first two elements.

Usefulness of the raking anti-picking pins

If you are making use of locks that is in possession of anti-picking pins, then this technique of raking will not produce results. These types of locks include serrated pins, spools, and mushroom pins.

When you find yourself in such situation, simply consider using the book pick, since it will let you to fully comprehend these anti-picking pins and even place them in the rightful manner.

In most cases, the pins located in a cylinder and that is in possession of the anti-picking pins are not all referred as anti-picking pins.

Also, despite the fact that all the pins are anti-picking pins, starting by false setting these anti-picking pins are necessary. After that, you can place them on the shear line in the rightful manner. This should be the scenario expect except for the fact that the key pin is regarded as an anti-picking pin.

Due to this, using a rake at the start of the picking process is useful, since it will be of assistance in setting the constant pins at the shear line and to also false set the anti-picking pins.

What is the preliminary action of making use of a rake on an anti-picking pin?

Well, you can use a feeler hook to set pins, but only if the anti-picking pins have been set at a false set and the plug rotated by some degrees.

Since tension tools requires to be released a bit to place the anti-picking pins, some of the pins placed at the shear line might not be placed properly.

You should still have the chance to make use of the two techniques to place a few of the pins by setting and raking any anti-picking pins with a feeler hook. You can alternate these two techniques till the lock is finally open.

Making Use of Single Pin picking tools

There are numerous forms of picking tools. You can pick tools from diamonds, hooks, or half moons. Keep in mind that these tools can all act in the same way on one pin at a time.

Applying the correct tension in the plug is the essential and critical aspect of single pin picking. Also, the correct tension that is applied in the plug can help to gradually set the pins at the shear line.

Just as we said earlier, the plug that is being tensioned is been blocked from rotating further by the pins that are already trapped between the shell and the plug.

Due to this, starting to set the first binding pin is very necessary. It can only be stopped or hindered by friction, since it has a higher chance of remaining placed at the shear line.

Once you are through with this, a new pin will be bonded by the friction, which can be determined by feedback through the pick to place the pin in the rightful manner. You continue to repeat this procedure till you have the cylinder opened. While this theory of making use of picking tool is very easy, you can have the practical use more complicated.

The brand and model determines the space available in the keyway. You should have a lot of bad feedback if you are using the narrow keyways. The reason is that the friction of your tool is certainly against the keyway.

You might find this technique complicated if you intend to acquire knowledge on placing your tool in the cylinder, especially on top of the pins to set them and upholding good feedback at the exact time.

You can also consider acquiring cutaway cylinder when you are in the beginning process of learning this technique. If you use this specific cylinder, then you might know how to place your pick on the pins. You should also know how to move ahead quickly by associating the action of the tool with the sensations given to you through the tool.

How to apply the appropriate tension when single pin picking

This particular topic has been closely monitored especially in the chapter on tensioning. Nonetheless, always remember that the ideal or perfect training for single pin picking is to tension from the bottom of the keyway while also checking that that the tension tool is not causing any hindrance on the movement of the first pin.

The required tension is rather applied with a short rigid tension tool to enable the plug rotate a few degrees from its restful position. If you want to create the required friction on the pins that is placed between the shell and the plug, then you need to consider this technique.

CHAPTER ELEVEN

Common Lock Picking Mistakes

Picking locks that are too hard

Even though it is important to challenge yourself in getting better, you should not be picking locks that you are yet to learn the skills or even developed senses. If you do, then you might get frustrated or even discourage yourself from picking locks.

You are supposed to experience fun when lock picking and the fastest method of getting better is by ensuring that it remains fun.

Below, there are two tips that can be of assistance in steering you in the right direction and making sure lock picking does not twist into frustration.

1. Have a Plan

Let us assume you are a novice, it is advisable to possess a rough plan of progression. Do not begin to use spool pins to pick locks till you are very comfortable with single pin picking standard pins.

It is also recommended you follow a lock progression guide. You might consider this guide known as the 'Nine Best Practice Locks to Learn Lock picking quickly'. It is not necessary for you to make use of the same locks, but knowing the type of locks you should be picking is what makes the difference.

In other words, building a house from the ground up is much easier than from the sky down.

2. Take 5

Let us assume you are stucked on a lock, the ideal thing you should consider is to take it one side before you get frustrated.

You can place the guide in a drawer or table for some days or even weeks. Then, practice on other kind of locks or even practice the easier ones to get a little motivation.

Keep in mind that the easiest locks can at times throw you a challenge you never thought about. In some situations, we may not be ready for the challenge a few locks have for us, and at times, we are not in the perfect state to pick these locks. Irrespective of this situation, assuming you are unable to pick a lock, simply go back to it after you must have gained some experience. You will be surprised at the outcome.

Improper Tools

One massive mistake a lot of people make especially when beginning is that they waste money on most affordable lock picking sets especially those ones you can see on Amazon.

If you must know, the lifespan of your picks can be affected by the quality of your lock picks. Not only that, the feedback they offer, and the entire effectiveness of your lock picks can be affected by the quality.

Lock Picking

Let us assume you opt for picks that are produced from poor material, then know that these materials can easily break, bend, or even rust. You would not be able to use the tool if you experience any of the following mentioned above.

An investment you can make is to go for a quality set. Even though a quality set is more expensive, it will be durable for a couple of years.

It is not compulsory for you to spend heavily on every picks referred to you. In fact, all what you need is just a couple of nice rakes, hooks, and a pleasant variety of tensioning tools.

The Peterson GSP Ghost set is a very good recommendation for people who are in search of their first quality lock pick set. Nonetheless, assuming you do not fancy this specific lock pick set, you can opt for a similar set especially in its setup.

Irrespective of the route you follow, make sure you invest in some lock picking tools that offer quality and avoid lock picks from Amazon.

Relying on Transparent Locks

The transparent locks are part of the biggest mistakes or errors a lot of people are making currently. As long as lock picking is not a visual craft, it is better not to train yourself to depend on visual cues, since it will take away the focus on getting better.

Let us assume you are a novice in lock picking and you are yet to invest in your first lock, you are recommended to consider the master lock guide since it will enlighten you than any other guide.

Also, assuming you intend to make use of a cutaway for practice, this is the best time to leave it.

Concentrating on too much Raking

The ability to open a lock very fast is certainly among the most fascinating aspects of lock picking, irrespective of whether you are new or a veteran. When it comes to raking, nothing plays more heavily into this desire.

Do not get yourself confused. If you want to develop yourself as a lock picker, then learn how to rake. Besides, knowing how to rake can take you far.

Let us assume you are a beginner and you concentrate too much on raking, you might falsely gauge where your level of skill truly is.

When you start to conquer locks either side, you might end up smashing up against locks that you will not be able to rake. A more refined level of skill in tension control and single pin picking that are yet to be developed will be demanded by these locks.

You will certainly feel discouraged if you are taken back to easier locks to process the essentials of single pin picking.

You will even feel more discouraged when you find it very difficult or unable to use the single pin picking to open the locks and you know that you can use a rake to open the locks within a few seconds.

The best suggestion you can follow is by placing a rake on the back burner and concentrating on single pin picking and tension control. You will be astonished on the level you will get yourself by concentrating on these two things.

Do Not Practice Constantly

Even though the basic locks will fall rapidly to your mighty picks, the security pins or other extra obstacles will need some expertise or ability and a more complicated understanding that practicing will enable one to deliver.

A lose it or use it activity is the lock picking. In other words, always keep on practicing. As long as you practice on a daily basis, even though it takes you only 15 minutes daily, you will certainly be building on the skills and conserving them. Remember, it was so difficult for you at the beginning stage to acquire the skills.

When you practice or take a few minutes of your time daily to learn lock picking, you will be surprised on how you will get better.

CONCLUSION

With this guide, you should be able to have an extensive overview of how you can operate a lock and how you can open it non-destructively.

Certainly, the mastery of other techniques like the impressioning, decoding, bumpkeys, and the umbrella picks are required if you are considering the professional practice of the lock manipulation.

If you are looking at the large range of tasks a professional locksmith must rally it is important for him or her to be in possession of a wide range of techniques in order to locate a satisfactory solution to any future challenges.

Someone who usually discerns the shortcomings or drawbacks of any specific technique is otherwise known as a true professional. Even though using the methods of fine lock manipulation is not totally convincing especially in terms of allowing the resale of a cylinder after launching it, you will shocked to discover that your customers will like to follow your recommendations especially when you launched their door without any damage.

A satisfied customer, on the other hand, will give good recommendations which will automatically extend the circle of your customer loyalty.

ABOUT THE AUTHOR

Joseph McKnight first and most powerful love has always been teaching. He graduated from New Jersey Institute of Technology's Science in 2017 and ever since; he has been interested by the interplay that links social trends and human values to developments in the technical world.

While he gained his bachelor degree at NJIT, Joseph also completed the History degree Program federated between the institution and Rutgers

University. Currently, Joseph is a member of the board of directors of the American division of TOOOL, The Open Organization of Lockpickers.

Joseph McKnight

Manufactured by Amazon.ca
Bolton, ON

40149897R00077